SEASON OF WONDER

LONG AWAITED PROMISES FULFILLED

STACEY WEEKS

This book was outlined with the assistance of AI technology. The author has expanded upon, refined, and revised upon these outlines to create the final text. The ideas, themes, and messages presented are the author's own, shaped through thoughtful collaboration with AI as a tool for brainstorming and inspiration.

ISBN: 978-1-7381668-2-4

Grace and Love Publishing

FREE SHORT STORIES
FREE SHORT STUDIES

CONTENTS

PART I
A SEASON OF HOPE
THE PROMISE OF THE MESSIAH

1

THE PROPHECY OF HOPE

READ ISAIAH 9:6-7

Hope can feel risky because disappointment lurks closely behind it. If you've ever faced disappointment, you know that it's easier to expect little and be pleasantly surprised than hope big and feel crushed. Hope and fear often tango, each fighting to lead our hearts.

Continuing to hope in a desperate situation can feel like the dangerous, more painful choice. But if we give up, we risk missing the miracle.

> "For to us a child is born,
> to us a son is given;

and the government shall be upon his shoulder,
and his name shall be called
Wonderful Counselor, Mighty God,
Everlasting Father, Prince of Peace.
Of the increase of his government and of peace
there will be no end,
on the throne of David and over his kingdom,
to establish it and to uphold it
with justice and with righteousness
from this time forth and forevermore.
The zeal of the Lord of hosts will do this.

— ISAIAH 9:6-7

The hope born in Jesus will never disappoint. Scripture tells us that when Jesus rules—and He will rule—it will be wonderful. He understands our weaknesses and needs, yet holds the power and authority of God. His rule will not be like any earthly leader. Our human leaders repeatedly disappoint us. Their leadership can be marked by imperfections, failures, or corruption. But Jesus will reign with true justice, righteousness, and peace. The Bible describes this coming Kingdom as a place where every wrong will be made right, where sorrow and suffering will cease, and where God's glory will shine forever.

The promise of this Savior is woven throughout Scripture. The prophets foretold of a Messiah who would rescue and restore God's people. This King will sit on David's throne and establish a kingdom that will never end. This King—our Hope—is Jesus. He is the fulfillment of all God's promises, the One who was to come and who will come again.

Jesus is the embodiment of every hope humanity has longed for: hope for peace, hope for healing, hope for justice, and hope for a world made whole. Under His reign, we will experience life as it was meant to be—a life filled with joy, security, and unending worship of our King.

This is our hope: Jesus has come. This is

our hope: Jesus is coming again. The first Advent—the birth of Christ in a manger—points us forward to the second Advent, the glorious return of Christ. Our hope is not just in a historical event but in a future reality. Jesus has already come to bring salvation, and He will come again to complete His redemptive work.

So we wait, but it is not in despair. We wait in expectation. We hold to the promise that a day is coming when Jesus will return, and He will gather His people. His Kingdom will be fully established. Every tear will be wiped away, and His perfect justice and love will be known by all. Until then, we pray, we watch, and we hope, for the King is coming soon.

REFLECTION

You'll find hope as you remember the Messiah was promised to you before you even knew you needed Him. As you read the prophecies, lean into God's promises. No matter what life throws your way, you can find comfort in knowing there's an eternal plan in motion. So, hold on to hope!

PRAYER

Heavenly Father, thank You for the promise of the Messiah. When I face challenges, remind me that Jesus is my Wonderful Counselor. In moments of weakness, redirect my mind to You, my Mighty God. When I feel alone, help me feel the love of You, my Everlasting Father. And in times of turmoil, grant me the peace that only the Prince of Peace can give. I want this season to be a time of renewed hope and a deeper trust in Your promises. Help me share this hope with those around me. In His precious name, I pray. Amen.

2

HOPE IN THE WAITING

READ MICAH 5:2-4

Micah was written hundreds of years before the birth of Jesus. In it, the people learn the Messiah will come from Bethlehem. He will be a shepherd to the flock. He will act in the strength of the Lord. He will bring security. He will be great.

> “But you, O Bethlehem Ephrathah,
> who are too little to be among the clans of Judah,
> from you shall come forth for me
> one who is to be ruler in Israel,
> whose coming forth is from of old,

from ancient days.
Therefore he shall give them up until the time
when she who is in labor has given birth;
then the rest of his brothers shall return
to the people of Israel.
And he shall stand and shepherd his flock in the strength of the Lord,
in the majesty of the name of the Lord his God.
And they shall dwell secure, for now he shall be great
to the ends of the earth.

— MICAH 5:2-4

Scholars say the people of Israel waited nearly 700 years for the fulfillment of Isaiah's prophecy. That's seven centuries of anticipation, longing, and questioning. It's difficult for us, on this side of history, to fully grasp what it must have been like for generation after generation to cling to this promise in the midst of political upheaval, exile, and silence from God. They must have wondered if they had misunderstood. Did God mean what He said? Was there a mistake?

Waiting can often feel like that—uncertain, uncomfortable, even agonizing. It's a space where doubts creep in, where hope thins, and impatience threatens to take over. And yet, throughout Scripture, God's people are continually called to wait. Not just to pass the time or sit idly, but to *actively* wait in faith, believing that what God has said will be, even when circumstances suggest otherwise.

Are you in a season of waiting right now? Are you waiting for God to fulfill a promise, to bring healing, to answer prayers? Perhaps you, too, feel a bit disappointed or confused, wondering if you've misheard or misunderstood. But remember this: God has not forgotten you. He does not delay without purpose. He is not constrained by time or circumstances. The same God who upheld His promise through centuries is the God who stands by you today. He is your solid rock, your fortress, and your ever-present help.

The challenge is to wait well—to wait with full confidence in God's character. His strength is unchanging, unshakeable, and eternal. His wisdom laid the earth's foundations; His understanding set the stars in place; and He upholds the universe. If His wisdom was sufficient to create the universe, won't it also be sufficient for your circumstances? His understanding will see you through your waiting.

The Lord is trustworthy. When we wait on Him, we are not left hanging by a thread that might break. We are grounded on a foundation that cannot be shaken. The waiting is not wasted. It shapes us, refines us, and deepens our trust in the One who holds our future. He will strengthen you. He will give you courage. And He will renew your hope. Though the fulfillment may seem far off, wait expectantly, because God is faithful. When the time was right, the promised Messiah was born in Bethlehem, just as God had said. And one day, in His time, He will fulfill every promise He made to you in His Word.

So wait with your soul anchored in His

promises. Wait in the assurance that He is working, even when you cannot see it. Wait, and let your heart find rest in Him alone. Those who wait on the Lord will never be put to shame.

REFLECTION

In what areas do you need to trust in God's timing even though it seems slow or uncertain? Are there promises you are waiting on? Situations where you feel uncertain or impatient? Just as God fulfilled His promise through the birth of Jesus in Bethlehem, He will fulfill His promises to you. Trust in His sovereignty and His plan for your life.

PRAYER

Heavenly Father, thank You for Your faithfulness and the promises You have given me. Help me to trust in Your timing, even when it seems slow or uncertain. Give me the patience and faith to wait on Your perfect plan. Remind me that You can bring beauty from ashes and that Your ways are higher than my ways. During this season, I want to find my hope and assurance in Your promises. Help me to share this hope with others. In Jesus' name, I pray. Amen.

3

THE FAITHFULNESS OF GOD

READ LAMENTATIONS 3:22-24

Many of our favorite Christmas carols sing the sound theology of God's faithfulness. They echo the never-changing melody of the Word of God. *Our hope is in the Lord.*

He puts a new song in our mouths, a song of praise to our God; many will see and fear and will trust in the Lord (Psalm 40:3). Like Moses, writing and teaching a song to the sons of Israel (Deut 31:22), at Christmas, our theology-rich carols remind a watching world that God is faithful.

No matter how tuneless the world's clanging grows, God is composing new morning mercies. All creation sings of His glory. Hearts ring out victory as He puts a new song in the mouths of His people. We sing our praises to Him and tell of His wondrous works. Our song is our witness.

A new heaven and new earth await. Today's Christmas melody preludes tomorrow's victory. The longing of our hearts and the upheaval of a nation prove that earth was never meant to be our victory song. One day, those who believe will join the angels in heaven and sing for all eternity of God's great faithfulness. We will sing our songs of repentance and dependence on Christ. We will sing with endless joy the song of the redeemed.

Sing of the new mercies God's given for this new day. Sing to our God, who is worthy to be praised. Sing to Him because we are His, known by name and redeemed. God is our hope. He is our salvation. This is our God. Praise Him (Exodus 15:2). Replace holly and tinsel lyrics with deep and meaningful verses. Learn these songs and sing of your hope. Sing to the Lord, all the earth (Psalm 33:3, Psalm 69:30, Psalm 96:1).[1]

> “The steadfast love of the Lord never ceases;
> his mercies never come to an end;
> they are new every morning;
> great is your faithfulness.
> “The Lord is my portion,” says my soul,
> “therefore I will hope in him.”
>
> — LAMENTATIONS 3:22-24

REFLECTION

When you declare, “The Lord is my portion,” you affirm that God is sufficient to meet all your needs. This season, embrace this reality and wait on the Lord with a hopeful heart. How can you actively place your hope in God’s faithfulness, even during challenging times? How can you share this hope with others who may be struggling?

PRAYER

Heavenly Father, thank You for Your unfailing love and compassion. In times of sorrow and hardship, help me to remember that Your mercies are new every morning and that Your faithfulness is great. Teach me to declare that You are my portion, trusting in Your sufficiency to meet all my needs. This season, fill my heart with hope and empower me to be a bearer of Your love and a light to those around me. May my life reflect Your goodness and bring encouragement to those who are struggling. In Jesus' name, I pray. Amen.

4

MARY'S HOPEFUL EXPECTATION

READ LUKE 1:26-38

We know the story. We know it so well that it's in danger of losing its wonder. Our busyness commemorating the holiday season combined with the cares of this world rub the shine off the narrative. If we're not careful, the opening lines of the biblical account will stir little more than the warm and fuzzy feelings of a fairy tale. We can be so consumed by the cares of this world that we miss the miracle of the season.

How many of us will miss seeing God because we are too busy to notice? How many of us don't hear His voice because we are listening to other voices instead? How many of us are so worried about the "what ifs" that we miss what God is doing?

Angels prepared Mary and Joseph for the unbelievable events about to unfold:

> "In the sixth month the angel Gabriel was sent from God to a city of Galilee named Nazareth, to a virgin betrothed to a man whose name was Joseph, of the house of David. And the virgin's name was Mary. And he came to her and said, "Greetings, O favored one, the Lord is with you!" But she was greatly troubled at the saying, and tried to discern what sort of greeting this might be. And the angel said to her, "Do not be afraid, Mary, for you have found favor with God. And behold, you will conceive in your womb and bear a son, and you shall call his name Jesus. He will be great and will be called the Son of the Most High. And the Lord God will give to him the throne of his father David, and he will

reign over the house of Jacob forever, and of his kingdom there will be no end.

— LUKE 1:26-33

As Mary received this amazing message of hope, the rest of the world carried on as usual. They travelled, made dinner, and fulfilled their daily obligations, unaware that God was about to change everything. In the midst of their ordinary lives, a miracle was quietly unfolding—one that would bring hope, not just for a single generation, but for all humanity.

And just as He was then, God is still at work today, often unseen and unnoticed, moving in ways we don't expect. While we go about our routines, God's promises remain true. He is still writing His story of hope, inviting us to lift our eyes and recognize His hand at work.

REFLECTION

Mary's response to the angel's message in verse 38, "I am the servant of the Lord; let it be to me according to your word," reflects a heart fully surrendered to the Lord's will. How can you demonstrate the same hope and trust in your life? What actions can you take to convey this hope and trust to those around you?

PRAYER

Thank You for Mary's example of hope and obedience. Her willingness to trust in Your plan despite the unknowns inspires me to place my faith in You. Give me eyes to see how you are working so I can be a vessel of Your hope, bringing encouragement and faith to my community. In Jesus' name, I pray. Amen.

5
THE BIRTH OF JOHN THE BAPTIST FORETOLD

READ LUKE 1:5-25

Sometimes, we can do everything right and still be unsuccessful. Zechariah and Elizabeth were both "righteous before God, walking blamelessly in all the commandments and statues of the Lord. But they had no child, because Elizabeth was barren, and both were advanced in years." Being childless was a great sorrow, especially since their culture viewed barrenness as judgment from God, yet, they walked *blamelessly*.

> In the days of Herod, king of Judea, there was a priest named Zechariah, of the division of

> Abijah. And he had a wife from the daughters of Aaron, and her name was Elizabeth. And they were both righteous before God, walking blamelessly in all the commandments and statutes of the Lord. But they had no child, because Elizabeth was barren, and both were advanced in years.
>
> — LUKE 1:5-7

It is possible to grieve great losses and still walk faithfully with God. Zechariah and Elizabeth are an example of this. Their story takes a miraculous turn when an angel foretells the birth of their son, John, who would prepare the way for the coming Messiah.

Though Zechariah and Elizabeth are described as "righteous" and "walking blamelessly" it is important to remember that they were not truly without sin. Other passages of Scripture tell us that "all have sinned and fall short of the glory of God" (Romans 3:23). Their blamelessness does not imply they were perfect, but rather that they lived faithfully according to God's law.

True blamelessness comes not from our own works but through Jesus Christ. It is only by being covered in His holiness and righteousness that anyone can stand righteous before God. Zechariah and Elizabeth's faithfulness pointed to their trust in God, but like all believers, they needed the grace and redemption offered by the coming Messiah.

REFLECTION

As you reflect on Zechariah and Elizabeth's faithfulness despite years of unfulfilled longing, think of your own longings. Resolve to trust God's character and His timing. Resist the temptation to allow bitterness or despair take root in your heart and, instead, trust God's goodness, even if His plan remains hidden. Take courage from their example. God hears your prayers, He sees your faithfulness, and He is faithful to bring about His purposes in your life. While you wait, let your hope rest not in the fulfillment of a specific desire but in the One who holds all things in His hands.

PRAYER

Heavenly Father, help me to trust in Your timing and remain steadfast in my faith, even when I face challenges. As I prepare for the celebration of Jesus' birth, may my heart be filled with hope and joy. In Jesus' name, I pray. Amen.

6

THE MAGNIFICAT: MARY'S SONG OF PRAISE

READ LUKE 1:46-55

In Luke 1:46-55, Mary's song of praise, known as the Magnificat, is an expression of hope. In these verses, Mary rejoices in God her Savior, contrasting her humble state with His mighty deeds. Despite the uncertainty surrounding her situation, Mary is filled with hope as she recounts all God has done.

> “And Mary said,
> My soul magnifies the Lord,
> and my spirit rejoices in God my Savior.
>
> — LUKE 1:46-47A

Mary's response to God's decision to involve her in the coming of the Messiah illustrates the power of worship and praise in uncertain circumstances. By choosing to worship, Mary shifted her focus from the challenges she faced to God's greatness. Remembering His past faithfulness reassured and strengthened her heart. It filled her with hope.

In our own times of uncertainty, worship declares our trust in God's plan. It invites us to recount His blessings, remember His character, and proclaim His mercy and justice.

REFLECTION

How can you incorporate intentional worship into your daily life? Consider the mighty deeds God has done for you and praise Him. Let this season be a time of joyful hope, where your spirit rejoices in God your Savior. Through worship, you can find strength and encouragement, reminding yourself and others of the hope you have in Christ.

PRAYER

Heavenly Father, help me to express my hope through worship and praise. Remind me of Your faithfulness and mighty deeds in my life. Fill my heart with joy and trust in Your promises, especially in times of uncertainty. May my worship be a testament to Your goodness and a source of encouragement for those around me. Cause my spirit to rejoice in You. In Jesus' name, I pray. Amen.

7
A PERSONAL REFLECTION ON HOPE

READ PSALM 33:20-22

“Our soul waits for the Lord;
he is our help and our shield.
For our heart is glad in him,
because we trust in his holy name.
Let your steadfast love, O Lord, be upon us,
even as we hope in you.

— PSALM 33:20-22

Hope is a central theme of the Christmas season. The story of Christ's birth is the fulfillment of a hope that began long before Jesus arrived in the manger. The Israelites had waited for centuries for the promised Messiah, clinging to the hope of God's promise. When we celebrate Christ's birth, we are celebrating the arrival of hope itself.

Hope is a powerful force. In Psalm 33:20-22, the psalmist is waiting on the Lord, trusting in His protection, and rejoicing in His holy name. This passage reminds us that our hope is not passive; it is active and filled with trust in God's unfailing love.

How has the hope of Christ's coming impacted you? Perhaps there were seasons of waiting and uncertainty, much like Mary and Joseph experienced before Jesus was born. Think about the times when you placed your hope in God and how that shaped your decisions, your outlook, and your emotions. Consider moments of waiting—perhaps for an answer to prayer, for a dream to be fulfilled, or for healing in a difficult situation. How did your hope in God sustain you during those times?

Hope is anchored in the truth of God's character. When we put our hope in the Lord, we acknowledge His sovereignty, His goodness, and His faithfulness. It encourages us to look beyond our current struggles and trust in God's greater plan. Let the celebration of Jesus' birth remind you that the same hope that sustained generations before you is alive and active in your life today.

Note specific instances where you hoped in God. How was He your help and shield? How did trusting in His name bring joy to your heart? How does remembering God's actions in the past encourage you as you wait on Him now? Reflect on His unfailing love and how it continues to give you hope.

PRAYER

Heavenly Father, thank You for the gift of hope that anchors my soul. As I reflect on Psalm 33:20-22, I am reminded of Your unfailing love and faithfulness. Help me to wait on You with an active, trusting hope. Bring to my mind the ways You have been my help and shield. Strengthen my hope in You, and let it shape my life for Your glory. In Jesus' name, I pray. Amen.

Hope

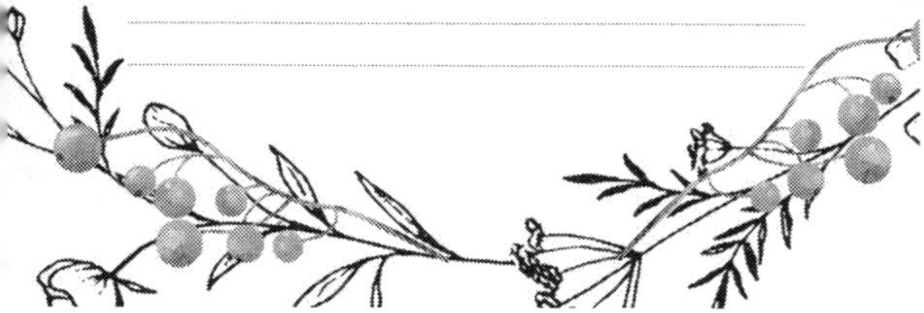

PART II
A SEASON OF PEACE

THE PEACE BROUGHT BY THE MESSIAH

8

THE PRINCE OF PEACE

READ ISAIAH 9:6

> “For to us a child is born, to us a son is given, and the government shall be upon his shoulder, and his name shall be called Wonderful Counselor, Mighty God, Everlasting Father, Prince of Peace.
>
> — ISAIAH 9:6

One of the names given to Jesus is the Prince of Peace. As the Prince of Peace, Jesus brings several kinds of peace to our lives.

Jesus brings peace with God. Through His sacrifice, He reconciles those who repent and believe to God, bridging the separation caused by sin (Rom 5:1). Jesus also brings inner peace. In a world full of anxiety and turmoil, He offers a peace that passes understanding (Phil 4:7). In addition to bringing peace with God and inner peace, Jesus teaches us to love our neighbors, to forgive those who wrong us, and, as much as it depends on us, live in peace with those around us (Rom 12:18).

Peace is more than an absence of anxiety, fear, and stress. It is a total trust in the Lord. Jesus, as the Price of Peace, offers a peace that is different from the peace of the world (John 14:27). It has to be because we needn't look far to see the world has no peace to give. Our flesh wants to believe that this type of peace is too hard. Our flesh wants to scramble after man-made solutions, but wisdom reminds us that God meets every need (Phil 4:19).

We know this. Now, we must live like we believe this. As we mentally fight for biblical thinking one day (one hour) at a time, we live and focus on this day, not worrying about tomorrow (Matt 6:34). This requires us to take every thought captive and make it obedient to Christ (2 Cor 10:5).

The full realization of the peace that Jesus brings will not be experienced until the new heaven and the new earth, where sin and death are defeated forever. In this kingdom, there will be no more sorrow, pain, or separation—only joy in the presence of the Prince of Peace who will reign forever.[1]

REFLECTION

When you commit your mind to the things of the Lord, peace follows. It is exhausting to continually redirect your thoughts but it is also freeing. Peace from God enables you to depend on the One who holds the answers, and that is why it can bring peace within circumstances that haven't changed. In what circumstance do you need to move your gaze from the trial to the Savior? He is worth more than anything this broken world promises. Let your heart not be troubled.

PRAYER

Heavenly Father, I thank You for the gift of Jesus, the Prince of Peace. As I reflect on Isaiah 9:6, I am grateful for the peace He brings into my life. Help me to fully embrace this peace in my relationship with You, finding wholeness and restoration. Grant me inner peace that transcends my understanding, especially in times of anxiety and uncertainty. Teach me to be peacemaker in my relationships with others. May the peace of Christ dwell richly in my heart and transform my life. In Jesus' name, I pray. Amen.

9

PEACE IN THE STORM

READ MARK 4:35-41

In Mark 4:35-41, the disciples are in a boat with Jesus, crossing to the other side of the Sea of Galilee. As they travel, a violent storm arises, threatening to capsize the boat. Despite being experienced fishermen, the disciples are overwhelmed with fear. Their fear is contrasted with Jesus, who is sleeping peacefully.

When the disciples wake Jesus in a panic, Jesus rebukes the wind and commands the waves to be still, and the storm immediately calms. Jesus then questions their fear and lack of faith. This entire exchange leaves the disciples grappling with a new fear.

> “And they were filled with great fear and said to one another, “Who then is this, that even the wind and the sea obey him?”
>
> — MARK 4:41

The disciples’ fear shifts from the storm to a reverent fear of Jesus. Initially terrified by the power of the wind and waves, they now stand in awe of the One who has authority over that wind and those waves. This transition from fearing their circumstances to fearing God is significant. This fear leads to reverence and worship of God that is similar to the awe that the shepherds felt when the angels proclaimed Christ’s birth.

When we replace our earthly fears with a fear of the Lord, we are reminded that He is greater than any trial we face. The Prince of Peace, whose birth we celebrate, is sovereign over all things. We will face storms as we walk the earthly path the Lord has ordained for us. Yet, just as Jesus was with the disciples in the boat, He is with us in our storms. His presence brings peace—not because everything around us is calm, but because He is the One who brings peace on earth and goodwill to all.

It would be easy to spiral downward with anxiety: Are we parenting right? Are the children learning everything they need to know? Do they know how desperately, wholeheartedly, and unconditionally we love them? Will we have enough money to retire? Should we be saving for college? Do we invest, pay down the mortgage, fix up the house, or just give it all away?

The anxiousness that filled the disciples was a symptom of a deeper problem. Their distracted hearts had ripped from their memory what Jesus had already said: They were going to *cross to the other side* (v35). If Jesus said they would cross to the other side, there was no storm that could sink their ship.

Jesus' rebuke to the disciples—"Why are you so afraid? Do you still have no faith?"—echoes to us as an invitation to trust Him more deeply this Christmas. When we fix our eyes on the One born in a manger, we experience a peace that surpasses all understanding. This season, let's celebrate not only His birth but also remember the words He has shared with us in Scripture. He is present in every storm and greater than any trial we face.

REFLECTION

What storms are you currently facing? How can you invite Jesus into those situations? What has He said in His Word that speaks truth into your anxiousness? Trusting Jesus means believing that His peace is available to you even when the winds are howling. Surrender your fears and rest in His power and love.

PRAYER

Heavenly Father, thank You for Your Son, who brings peace in the midst of life's storms. Help me to trust in Your presence and power, even when I feel overwhelmed. Teach me to surrender my fears and to rest in Your unfailing love. Strengthen my faith, that I may find peace and calm in You regardless of my circumstances. In Jesus' name, I pray. Amen.

10

PEACE WITH GOD

READ ROMANS 5:1-2

> “Therefore, since we have been justified through faith, we have peace with God through our Lord Jesus Christ. Through him we have obtained access by faith into this grace in which we stand, and we rejoice in hope of the glory of God.
>
> — ROMANS 5:1-2

Paul's message of peace through Jesus Christ takes on special meaning during the Christmas season. As we celebrate the birth of Jesus, we remember that He came to bring peace—not just an absence of conflict or a feeling of calm; but peace that reconciles us to God.

When the angels announced Jesus' birth to the shepherds, they declared, *"Glory to God in the highest, and on earth peace among those with whom he is pleased!"* (Luke 2:14). This is more than a sentiment of holiday cheer. God ripped open the heavens so the angels could proclaim that salvation had come.

This flesh-wrapped Deity bears the brokenness suffocating you and me. He pieces us back together with His perfection. He doesn't always change our circumstances, but He always changes us. Christ has come, and He invites us to follow Him from the manger all the way to the cross—where a weary world can finally lay its burden down.

It's through faith in Jesus that we are justified, meaning we are seen as righteous by God. This justification brings us into a state of peace with God.

Before Christ's arrival, sin separated humanity from God. But on that first Christmas, God's answer to our problem was a tiny baby born in Bethlehem. Christmas proves that God knows our greatest need. Christmas is God making a way out from under the heap of wrath poured onto all sinners. Christmas is our way through the hardships.

Through Jesus' life, death, and resurrection, Jesus would tear down the barrier between us and God. The manger points forward to the cross, where Jesus took upon Himself the punishment for our sins and, in exchange, offered us His righteousness. Now, those who have put their faith in Him are justified—declared righteous in God's sight. This is the true peace of Christmas: peace *with* God.

Celebrate the peace with God that Jesus brings. The baby wrapped in swaddling clothes is more than a symbol of hope—He was and is our peace.[1]

REFLECTION

How does Jesus' sacrifice bring you peace with God? How does this peace affect your daily life, your interactions with others, and your perspective on challenges? This peace is a gift that transforms you, grounding you in the hope of God and empowering you to live out your faith with confidence and joy.

PRAYER

Heavenly Father, thank You for the gift of peace through the Lord Jesus Christ. I am grateful for the justification that comes by faith and for the grace in which I now stand. Help me to fully grasp the depth of Your love as I reflect on Jesus' sacrifice. Help me grow in my understanding and appreciation of the peace I have with You that came at a great cost. In Jesus' name, I pray. Amen.

11

ANGELS ANNOUNCE PEACE

READ LUKE 2:8-14

"And in the same region there were shepherds out in the field, keeping watch over their flock by night. And an angel of the Lord appeared to them, and the glory of the Lord shone around them, and they were filled with great fear. And the angel said to them, "Fear not, for behold, I bring you good news of great joy that will be for all the people. For unto you is born this day in the city of David a Savior, who is Christ the Lord. And this will be a sign for you: you will find a baby wrapped in swaddling cloths and lying in a manger." And suddenly there was with the angel a multitude of the heavenly host praising God and saying,

"Glory to God in the highest,
and on earth peace among those with whom he is pleased!"

Luke 2:8-14

The world could use some peace. It longs for a silent night. A single night without bombing, attacks, or viruses. It needs calm, and the whole world groans with longing.

Instead of quiet we hear shouting. We feel rage and anxiety. We live in chaos and anguish. It's in the papers. Social media. Broadcasts. Groaning.

So much anger and fear.

Our souls could use some peace. We long for the sweet rest of the beloved. But this present time keens with suffering, aching to usher in hope's conclusion that began one bright and holy night. This peace arrived with the moaning and pains of childbirth. It slipped out of a womb and into our sorrow, unassuming and humble. Heavenly peace.

How is it possible for heavenly peace to arrive amid political turmoil and religious unrest? How is it possible for heavenly peace to soothe our souls amid instability and conflict? Yet, this is how the Prince arrives. And He sleeps, so the song says, in heavenly peace.

The announcement of Christ's birth to the shepherds is one of the most powerful moments in the Christmas story. Simple shepherds were the first to hear the angelic proclamation of peace. In the quiet fields, as they tended their sheep, the heavens erupted with glorious news: the long-awaited Messiah had come.

The Messiah sleeps in a manger, completely secure that teenaged Mary and inexperienced Joseph will fulfill their roles in His earthly story. He sleeps in peace as the heavens declare the glory of God in an angelic display and shepherds fall to their knees in awe. He sleeps in peace as the Maji set out on a two-year journey that will change their lives. He sleeps in peace as a massacre meant to destroy Him begins, and those wide-eyed teenagers follow supernatural instructions to flee.

Heavenly peace. And He offers it to us.

Peace, not as the world gives, but the kind only He can give. A peace that anticipates a holy day when creation will be set free from its bondage to corruption. A peace that knows the glory that is to be revealed will surpass all the hardship.

But this peace is far deeper than the end of wars. It is the peace that comes from God's favor, a peace that rests on those who receive Christ. The peace proclaimed to the shepherds is the same peace offered to us today: peace with God, peace within ourselves, and peace with others.

We can sleep in peace despite the wars, despite the viruses, despite all that is wrong in this world because our King has promised us one day the groaning will end. One day, the babe that came in peace, died in violence, and rose in victory will return in triumph. This Prince of Peace will bring the peace of God to every knee that bows and every tongue that confesses Jesus is Lord.[1]

REFLECTION

In what areas do you need to experience the peace that Jesus brings? How can you share this peace with those around you? Just as the shepherds were transformed by the angelic announcement, you too can be transformed by the peace that Christ offers.

PRAYER

Heavenly Father, I thank You for the gift of Your Son, Jesus, and for the peace He brings to my life. As I reflect on the angels' message to the shepherds, help me to embrace the peace that comes from knowing You. May this peace calm my heart in times of uncertainty. Help me to rest in the peace that only Christ can give. In Jesus' name, I pray. Amen.

12

LIVING IN PEACE

READ PHILIPPIANS 4:4-9

“Rejoice in the Lord always; again I will say, rejoice. Let your reasonableness be known to everyone. The Lord is at hand; do not be anxious about anything, but in everything by prayer and supplication with thanksgiving let your requests be made known to God. And the peace of God, which surpasses all understanding, will guard your hearts and your minds in Christ Jesus.

Finally, brothers, whatever is true, whatever is honorable, whatever is just, whatever is pure,

> whatever is lovely, whatever is commendable, if there is any excellence, if there is anything worthy of praise, think about these things. What you have learned and received and heard and seen in me—practice these things, and the God of peace will be with you.
>
> — PHILIPPIANS 4:4-9

As we celebrate the birth of Christ, we remember that He is *"Emmanuel"—God with us.* This is why Paul could say, *"Rejoice, for the Lord is at hand."* Paul doesn't ignore the reality of difficulties but instead offers a practical solution for how to live in peace.

It's natural to feel anxious when life becomes overwhelming. We all face circumstances that test our peace—whether it's financial pressures, health concerns, relationship struggles, or personal disappointments. But Paul's message encourages us to not let anxiety rule. Instead, we are to turn to God with our needs, thanking Him for what He has already done, and trusting Him with the future.

Managing our circumstances will never bring lasting peace—the darkness and pervasiveness of sin roots far too deep for that. Instead, peace comes with an understanding that God uses the hard events of life to accomplish far more extraordinary things than He would by removing difficulty. And the promise is clear: when we surrender our worries to God, His peace WILL guard our hearts and minds. This peace sustains us even when circumstances don't improve. It's a peace that reassures us that God is in control, no matter how chaotic things feel.

Just as the wise men rejoiced at the sight of the star and the shepherds praised God for what they had seen, we are called to dwell on what is true, honorable, just, pure, lovely, and worthy of praise. We make a choice to trust Him when we yield control to him. A wise woman once said, "We find the peace of God offered in verse seven, when we know the God of peace mentioned in verse nine."[1]

In practical terms, this looks like beginning each day with prayer, releasing our anxieties to God, and remembering His faithfulness. It looks like cultivating gratitude, even in the small things, and practicing contentment in all situations. When we focus on Christ's presence rather than on our problems, we are reminded that the Prince of Peace reigns over every circumstance.

Instead of being ruled by fear or stress, we remember that God is with us. His peace guards us, protecting our hearts from despair and our minds from confusion. This peace becomes a witness to others, showing the world that true peace is found in Christ alone.

REFLECTION

How can you practically live out the peace of God in your daily life? Are there areas of anxiety that you need to surrender to God? How can you make prayer and thanksgiving a regular part of your life, so that His peace can flow through you? Trust that the peace of God will guard your heart and mind, as you rest in Him.

PRAYER

Lord Jesus, thank You for the gift of Your peace. I surrender my anxieties to You and trust in Your perfect plan for my life. Help me to live in daily peace, turning to You in prayer and thanksgiving, no matter what I face. Guard my heart and mind, and let Your peace transform how I live and respond to the challenges around me. In Your name I pray, Amen.

13

BE A PEACEMAKER

READ MATTHEW 5:9

> “Blessed are the peacemakers, for they will be called sons of God.
>
> — MATTHEW 5:9

In the Sermon on the Mount, Jesus calls His followers to be peacemakers and says those who pursue peace will be known as children of God. This challenges us to go beyond pursuing and enjoying peace in our own lives. We are to actively create peace in the world around us. We are to be peacemakers.

Jesus stepped into our broken world to bring healing and reconciliation, and we are to step into places of brokenness, tension, and discord and bring peace. It's intentional. A peacemaker enters places of conflict and division. They enter uncomfortable situations to speak words of truth and show kindness and grace in difficult circumstances. They value unity in relationships and communities, and choose to resolve differences in a Christlike way.

But how do we do this in a world filled with tension, anger, and discord? Our ability to be peacemakers flows from our relationship with Jesus, the Prince of Peace. We become instruments of His peace when we allow Him to shape how we interact with others. We can extend grace to others because we recognize the grace that has been extended to us.

The Christmas season often brings us into contact with family members, friends, or communities where differences and old wounds may exist. When we are peacemakers, we choose not to escalate a tense situation. We offer a listening ear and extend forgiveness because our responses have the power to either draw others to the

Lord or drive them away. How we represent Christ matters.

REFLECTION

Think about your community. Where can you bring peace? Is there a relationship in need of mending? Are there places of tension in your workplace, home, or neighborhood? Ask God to show you how you can be a peacemaker, and trust Him to guide your steps as you seek to bring harmony and unity.

PRAYER

Heavenly Father, help me to be a peacemaker in my community. I want to reflect Your love and grace in my interactions with others. Give me the courage to step into conflict with a heart of reconciliation. Guide my words and actions so that I promote unity and understanding. I want to be known as Your child, sharing the peace of Christ with a world that desperately needs it. In Jesus' name, I pray. Amen.

14
A PERSONAL REFLECTION ON PEACE

READ COLOSSIANS 3:15

> “And let the peace of Christ rule in your hearts, to which indeed you were called in one body. And be thankful.
>
> — COLOSSIANS 3:15

Paul’s encouragement to the church to “let the peace of Christ rule” in their hearts is a good word for us. In our fast-paced world, filled with conflicting voices and anxieties, it’s easy for our hearts to be ruled by fear, anger, or worry. We might even be tempted to manipulate a false sense of peace through controlling our environment. Yet true peace comes only when Christ is the center of our hearts and minds.

Think back to moments in your life where Christ's peace carried you through challenging or uncertain times. Perhaps it was during a period of loss, stress, or fear when, despite everything, you felt an inner sense of calm and trust that God was in control.

What was it like to feel that peace? How did it change your perspective? How did that peace influence your actions or relationships during that season?

Paul's words are not just about receiving peace; it is about allowing that peace to influence how we live and interact with those around us. If Christ's peace rules in our hearts, it will impact our thoughts, words, and actions. It will shape how we respond to conflict, how we forgive, and how we show grace and love to others.

The peace we carry as followers of Christ is a powerful testimony in a world filled with anxiety, division, and turmoil. You might share this peace through offering forgiveness in a strained relationship, reaching out to someone who is hurting, or being a calming presence in a chaotic circumstance. What would it look like to let God's peace guide your responses, thoughts, and interactions in these areas?

Just as the birth of Christ was an expression of God's desire to restore peace between Himself and humanity, we are called to be messengers of peace, bringing it into our families, workplaces, and communities. So, this Christmas, as you reflect on the peace that Christ offers, consider how you can be an agent of that peace—a calming presence, a source of grace, and a reminder of the Prince of Peace who came to dwell among us.

PRAYER

Lord Jesus, thank You for the peace You have given me. Show me how I can share Your peace with others. Guide me to live in a way that reflects the unity and peace You have called me to as a member of Your family. In Your precious name, I pray. Amen.

Peace

PART III

A SEASON OF JOY

THE JOY OF THE MESSIAH'S COMING

15

JOY FORETOLD

READ ISAIAH 35:10

> “And the ransomed of the Lord shall return
> and come to Zion with singing;
> everlasting joy shall be upon their heads;
> they shall obtain gladness and joy,
> and sorrow and sighing shall flee away.
>
> — ISAIAH 35:10

The prophet Isaiah speaks of a future where those who are rescued by the Lord will sing and experience joy. The joy he describes is an *everlasting joy*. This joy will overtake sorrow and sighing. It will overwhelm the Lord's children in the most wonderful way. When we celebrate Jesus' birth, we are celebrating the arrival of the One who brings everlasting joy to all who believe.

For those of us who have experienced the redemption of Christ, this joy is not only a future certainty—it is also a present reality. We can live in the joy of God's promises now, even in the midst of difficulties and disappointments. We still experience sorrow, but we know it will one day be replaced with unending joy. So we hold onto that promise and believe that God's rescue plan is at work, even when we cannot see it fully.

The joy foretold by Isaiah is rooted in the faithfulness of God. This kind of joy comes from trusting in His promises and believing that He will bring us through every trial. This joy allows us to live with hope, not just for the future, but for today. God is with us.

Jesus is the fulfillment of Isaiah's prophecy—the One who brings everlasting joy. Jesus fills our hearts with a joy that is present and eternal. Jesus brought joy to the world.

REFLECTION

How can you live in the joy of God's promises today? Is there a present sorrow that weighs on you? Ask God to help you believe that it will one day be replaced with joy.

PRAYER

Lord, thank You for the promise of everlasting joy through Your Son, Jesus Christ. Help me to live in the joy of Your redemption every day, trusting in Your promises even when life is difficult. As I celebrate the birth of Christ, fill my heart with gladness and hope, knowing that Your love never fails and Your grace is always sufficient. Remind me that the joy You give is rooted in the unchanging truth of who You are. In moments of weariness or disappointment, help me to fix my eyes on Jesus, the source of true and everlasting joy. May His joy be my strength today and always. In Jesus' name, Amen.

16

JOY IN JESUS' BIRTH

READ LUKE 2:10-11

> "And the angel said to them, "Fear not, for behold, I bring you good news of great joy that will be for all the people. For unto you is born this day in the city of David a Savior, who is Christ the Lord."
>
> — LUKE 2:10-11

The angel's announcement of Jesus' birth is one of the most joy-filled moments in Scripture. It wasn't a royal proclamation made from a palace balcony to the elite of society. It was a message of good news delivered to simple shepherds.

The long-awaited promise of God was fulfilled, and the heavens erupted in a joy that wasn't just for those shepherds or for the people of Israel. This joy is for "all the people," for the entire world, and for us today. This is the heart of the gospel—the good news of Jesus is for everyone.

This joy is not a rise of emotion tied to Christmas traditions, although those traditions might bring us joy. The joy of Christ's birth celebrates a world forever changed by God's love. Jesus came to us to make a way for us to experience eternal life with Him.

Christ's birth is a cause for joy because it means God is not a distant, far away God. He is *Immanuel*, God with us. He came down to walk among us, to be with us, and to live with us. He experienced life with us. The good, the bad, the easy and the hard. We are known, loved, and never alone. That is the joy that fills our hearts at Christmas. And it echoes long after the decorations are put away.

REFLECTION

When has Jesus drawn near to you in powerful ways? With whom can you share that experience? Let the message of the angel, "I bring you good news of great joy that will be for all the people," fill your heart and overflow to those around you. This joy is meant to be shared.

PRAYER

Heavenly Father, thank You for Jesus, whose birth brings me great joy and hope. Help me to meditate on this good news and let it fill my heart with joy, no matter my circumstances. I want to carry this joy into my daily life and share it with those around me so that others may also experience the wonder of Your love and salvation. In Jesus' name, I pray. Amen.

17

JOY IN THE PRESENCE OF JESUS

READ MATTHEW 2:10-11

> "When they saw the star, they rejoiced exceedingly with great joy. And going into the house, they saw the child with Mary his mother, and they fell down and worshiped him. Then, opening their treasures, they offered him gifts, gold and frankincense and myrrh.
>
> — MATTHEW 2:10-11

The Magi traveled from afar, guided by a star, with one singular purpose: to worship the newborn King.

When they saw the star resting over the place where Jesus was, Scripture tells us that they "rejoiced exceedingly with great joy."

This joy is the natural response to encountering Jesus. When the Magi entered the house, they bowed down in worship, recognizing that the child before them was the long-awaited Messiah.

Just like the Magi, we are invited to seek Jesus. And when we find Him, the joy of His presence fills us in ways that nothing else in the world can. Worldly joy might invite us to snuggle by the fire pursuing the promise of a wonderful life. But when we search 34th Street for a miracle that can only be found in a manger, we are left wanting. The joy we long for is found only in Jesus.[1]

The Magi's response was not only one of joy but also of worship and giving. They offered gifts to Jesus—gold, frankincense, and myrrh. In the same way, our response to the joy of knowing Jesus should be worship and the offering of our lives to Him. Whatever you do, do all to the glory of God (1 Cor 10:31).

REFLECTION

Have you taken the time to seek Jesus, not just in moments of need, but in every day of your life? Have you considered what it would look like to live your life for Him? Does the joy of His presence fill your heart and lead you to a place of worship and surrender? What fills your typical day? What would it look like to complete your tasks to the glory of God? Just as the Magi bowed before Jesus, you are invited to bow your heart before Him in awe and adoration.

PRAYER

Lord Jesus, thank You for the joy that comes from being in Your presence. Like the Magi, I come before You in worship, filled with awe that you love me. Help me to seek You with all my heart, and let the joy of knowing You overflow into all areas of my life. I want to respond to Your love with worship and offer you my life. In Your precious name, I pray. Amen.

18

REJOICING IN SALVATION

READ LUKE 1:67-79

“ And his father Zechariah was filled with the Holy Spirit and prophesied, saying,

“Blessed be the Lord God of Israel, for he has visited and redeemed his people ...

... to give knowledge of salvation to his people

in the forgiveness of their sins,

because of the tender mercy of our God,

whereby the sunrise shall visit us from on high...”

— LUKE 1:67-68, 77-78

After months of silence due to his disbelief, Zechariah's first words were words of praise, "Blessed be the Lord ..." he said. He celebrated the role his son John would play in preparing the way for Jesus and celebrated the coming salvation that Jesus would bring.

Zechariah rejoices because God's promise to redeem His people was being fulfilled. God "has come to His people and redeemed them." Salvation is not a distant hope but a present reality. Through Jesus, God's people experience the forgiveness of sins and a new life of peace.

There is a joy that comes from knowing that God's promises are true. Just as Zechariah celebrated the fulfillment of God's plan, we too can rejoice that salvation is ours. Through Jesus, we can be redeemed, forgiven, and brought into the light of God's love and mercy.

REFLECTION

Salvation is not only about receiving forgiveness, but it includes living in the freedom and hope that Jesus brings. No matter what you face, you are loved, saved, and secure in the arms of a faithful God if you have trusted in Jesus for the forgiveness of your sins. This gives you a reason to rejoice, not just in the future hope of heaven but in the daily reality of His presence.

How does the fulfillment of God's promises in Christ bring joy to your heart? How can you live in that joy daily? Let this season be a time of deep reflection and rejoicing in the salvation that has come through Jesus.

PRAYER

Heavenly Father, thank You for the joy of salvation and the fulfillment of Your promises in Jesus. Just as Zechariah rejoiced in Your mercy and redemption, I too praise You for the gift of salvation through Christ. Help me to live in the joy of Your love, knowing that I am forgiven and redeemed. I rejoice in all that You have done for me, and I want to share the hope and joy of salvation with those around me. In Jesus' name, Amen.

19

JOY THROUGH THE HOLY SPIRIT

READ GALATIANS 5:22-23

> “But the fruit of the Spirit is love, joy, peace, patience, kindness, goodness, faithfulness, gentleness, self-control; against such things there is no law.
>
> — GALATIANS 5:22-23

During the Christmas season, many things bring us joy. We delight in family gatherings, the beauty of twinkling lights, and the excitement of giving and receiving gifts. Even simple pleasures like sipping a warm cup of cocoa by the fire or hearing a beloved carol can lift our spirits.

But if we only seek joy in these types of moments, we risk missing the deeper, lasting joy that comes from celebrating the arrival of Christ.

The joy described in Galatians 5 is far greater than what holiday traditions can offer. It's the same joy that stirred in the hearts of the wise men as they saw the star that led them to the newborn King (Matthew 2:10). This joy isn't tied to perfect holidays, fulfilled expectations, or even to the absence of hardship. Instead, it's anchored in the One who came to dwell among us.

Consider the churches in Macedonia, which were filled with an abundance of joy even in extreme poverty and severe trials (2 Corinthians 8:2), or the Thessalonians, who received the word with joy despite much affliction (1 Thessalonians 1:6). Their joy wasn't based on their circumstances; it flowed from a heart fixed on Christ. The same joy is available to us today through the Holy Spirit. It's a joy that remains steady even when life is uncertain. It's a joy that can flourish even in difficulty.

This is the joy James calls us to count during trials (James 1:2). It is a gift that God gives us through His Holy Spirit. It's a fruit that grows in the lives of those who walk closely with the Spirit. The joy spoken of in Galatians is an abiding joy that flows from the presence of God within us.[1]

This Christmas, let's invite the joy of Christ to fill our hearts—not just in the beautiful moments, but in the challenging ones as well. Just as Christ brought hope, peace, and salvation through His birth, the Holy Spirit now brings joy into our lives as we walk in relationship with God. And when December ends, this joy will remain because Christ has come, and His Spirit is still at work in us.

REFLECTION

How can you experience more of this joy in your life? Are there areas where you need to rely more fully on the Holy Spirit to produce joy in your heart? As you prepare for the celebration of Christ's birth, invite the Spirit to cultivate joy in you, even in difficult or uncertain times. This joy, given by the Holy Spirit, can be a source of strength, hope, and peace as you reflect on God's faithfulness. You can rejoice in the knowledge that God is with you and working in your heart through His Spirit.

PRAYER

Lord, I thank You for the joy You produce in my heart. As I reflect on the coming of Christ, help me to experience the fullness of Your joy, no matter what I am going through. Teach me to rely on the Holy Spirit's presence in my life, trusting that You are at work, growing the fruit of the Spirit in me. May my joy be a witness to others of Your love and faithfulness. In Jesus' name, Amen.

20

JOY IN TRIALS

READ JAMES 1:2-4

> "Count it all joy, my brothers, when you meet trials of various kinds, for you know that the testing of your faith produces steadfastness. And let steadfastness have its full effect, that you may be perfect and complete, lacking in nothing.
>
> — JAMES 1:2-4

Jesus' birth didn't occur in comfort or ease—it took place in a smelly stable during the chaos of a Roman census. Yet that night was marked by joy that spread from the angels to the shepherds and beyond because Christ's arrival changed everything. And the same God who sent His Son back then is the One who walks beside us in every hardship today.

For many of us, the Christmas season is filled with celebrations, gatherings, and joyful moments. But it can also be a time of personal trials and heartache for many. For some, the season is marked by loneliness, grief, or the weight of unmet expectations. It's a bittersweet reminder that hardship, sorrow, and grief don't pause for the holidays.

Yet, even in these times, we are called to joy. In his letter, James tells us to "count it all joy" when we face various trials. James' instruction to count trials and the testing of our faith as joy makes little sense until he explains. He writes in verse 3 that the testing of faith, the developing of perseverance, and perseverance finishing its work will make us mature and complete, lacking in nothing, enabling us to receive the prize. We don't merely desire to survive our trials, we want to endure our suffering in such a way that we earn the prize that matters: the crown of life (James 1:12).

James is pointing us to a joy that goes

beyond temporary happiness. It has nothing to do with perfect holiday circumstances, and everything to do with the unchanging presence and purpose of Christ in our lives.[1]

May this Christmas be a time to see beyond the lights and traditions. True joy is not found in perfect celebrations, but in the presence of a perfect Savior. As we walk through trials this season, may we cling to the promise that God is with us—Immanuel, our source of unshakable joy.

REFLECTION

Consider the trials you are facing right now. How can you shift your perspective to see them as opportunities for growth and deeper reliance on God? The same God who sent His Son into the world to redeem you is with you in every trial, giving you the strength to persevere and joy that transcends your circumstances.

PRAYER

Lord, thank You for the joy that comes even in the midst of trials. Help me to trust in You when life is difficult, knowing that You are using these trials to strengthen my faith and develop perseverance. Teach me to find joy in the process of growth, confident that You are with me. Your joy is my true source of hope. In Jesus' name, Amen.

21

A PERSONAL REFLECTION ON JOY

READ 1 PETER 1:8-9

> "Though you have not seen him, you love him. Though you do not now see him, you believe in him and rejoice with joy that is inexpressible and filled with glory, obtaining the outcome of your faith, the salvation of your souls.
>
> — 1 PETER 1:8-9

Peter writes about a joy that is inexpressible and filled with glory. This joy fills the hearts of believers even though we have not seen Jesus with our physical eyes. This joy flows from faith—our deep belief in who Jesus is and what He has done for us. This joy flows from a place of thankfulness to God for stepping into our world to save us from our sin.

Take a moment to reflect on your journey with Christ. When have you experienced this kind of joy in your walk with Him? Perhaps it was in a moment of answered prayer, a time when you felt God's presence in a powerful way, or simply the quiet assurance of His love and grace. Thank God for that joy.

Cultivate more joy by spending time in reflection, recalling the ways God has been faithful to you. When we intentionally remember God's goodness, we are reminded that He is with us, working in our lives, and that the promise of our salvation is secure. This reflection fuels more joy and keeps us anchored in Christ.

Another way to nurture joy is to focus on gratitude. Joy grows in the soil of thankfulness. When we choose to give thanks, even in difficult seasons, we position our hearts to receive the joy that the Holy Spirit brings. Gratitude shifts our perspective from what we lack to what we have in Christ, and this perspective is key to experiencing the fullness of joy.

What joys have you encountered in your walk with Jesus? When has His presence filled you with peace and hope? How can you create space to experience more of that joy this Christmas and beyond? Through prayer, reflection, and gratitude, you can cultivate the kind of lasting joy that Peter describes—one that is rooted in your faith and in the salvation you have received through Christ.

PRAYER

Heavenly Father, thank You for the inexpressible joy that comes from knowing and loving Jesus. Help me to cultivate joy in my daily life by staying close to You. Teach me to live with a heart full of gratitude, knowing that my salvation in Christ is secure. In Jesus' name, Amen.

Joy

PART IV
A SEASON OF LOVE
THE FULFILLMENT OF HOPE, PEACE, AND JOY

22

IMMANUEL: GOD WITH US

READ MATTHEW 1:22-23

"All this took place to fulfill what the Lord had spoken by the prophet:

"Behold, the virgin shall conceive and bear a son,

and they shall call his name Immanuel"

(which means, God with us).

— MATTHEW 1:22-23

The name Immanuel, meaning "God with us," reminds us that the birth of Jesus was the coming of God Himself to dwell among us. In Jesus, God stepped into our world. He entered our struggles, joys, fears, and hopes to be present with us in a tangible and life-changing way.

The reality of *Immanuel* means that we are never alone. When we face challenges, uncertainties, or moments of deep need, we find comfort in knowing that God is with us. He came not only to rescue us from sin but to be present with us in the most intimate and personal way.

Jesus lived an earthly life, physically close to God's people. That means he fully understands our pain, grief, and fears. God's desire for closeness didn't end with Jesus' earthly ministry. Jesus eventually returned to the Father's side, but He did not leave us alone. He sent the Holy Spirit to be our Comforter, Helper, and Guide—and He called this good (John 16:7). Through the presence of the Holy Spirit, we can experience God's peace, guidance, and companionship daily. God's presence and intimacy with His people are ongoing and deeply personal. We have Immanuel—God with us—today, tomorrow, and forevermore.

The constant presence of God changes everything. In our darkest moments, God is with us. In our times of joy, He celebrates with us. And in the everyday moments, we find peace and purpose because God is there with us. The coming of Christ and the giving of the Holy Spirit display God's desire to remain close to His people. Jesus walked with God's children and redeemed us from sin. The Holy Spirit lives within God's children, making it possible for us to walk in step with God.

REFLECTION

How can you experience more of God's presence in your life? Perhaps it's through quiet moments of prayer, reflection on Scripture, and worship. Whatever it may be, let the name Immanuel remind you that God's presence is constant, and His love is always with you.

PRAYER

Father, thank You for being Immanuel, God with us. Help me to fully grasp the wonder of

Your nearness and celebrate the reality that You are always with me. As I reflect on the birth of Christ, fill my heart with the joy and peace that comes from knowing that I am never alone. In Jesus' name, Amen.

23
LOVE MADE CLEAR IN JESUS

READ 1 JOHN 4:9-11

> “In this the love of God was made manifest among us, that God sent his only Son into the world, so that we might live through him. In this is love, not that we have loved God but that he loved us and sent his Son to be the propitiation for our sins. Beloved, if God so loved us, we also ought to love one another.
>
> — 1 JOHN 4:9-11

At the heart of Christmas is the incredible truth that God’s love was manifested in Jesus. Manifested means *to be made clear*. The birth of Christ is more than just the arrival of a baby; it makes clear God's great love for us. God put on skin and stooped to earth to speak to us face-to-face because He loves us. God expressed His love in a way that we could see, touch, and experience.

Every aspect of Jesus' life reflects the depth of God's love for us. Christ not only demonstrates God's love but provides the way for us to be reconciled to God. It is through Jesus' death and resurrection that we can live, now and forever, in the presence of our holy God.

This love is not based on our ability to earn or deserve it. As John writes, "not that we loved God, but that He loved us." God initiates the relationship. He reaches out to us when we are far from Him.

We are called to respond to this love. Just as the angels announced the good news of Jesus' birth to shepherds who then spread that joy to others, God's love in Christ is not something to be kept for ourselves. John reminds us, "Since God so loved us, we also ought to love one another." Jesus set the example of what true love looks like. It's sacrificial and overflows to others. So as we celebrate Christ's birth and eventual sacrifice, we should be so overwhelmed by God's love that we eagerly share it with a world in need of the hope, peace, and joy He brings.

At Christmas, we remember the incredible gift of love that God has given us in Jesus. But it is also a time to intentionally consider how we can share that love with those in need of hope, encouragement, and compassion. Just as the shepherds couldn't keep the news of Christ's birth to themselves, our hearts should be so filled with His love that it overflows into the lives of those around us.

Reach out to those who might feel forgotten, and point them to the light that first broke through the darkness in Bethlehem. Let this Christmas season be marked by our response to God's love—a response that shares the good news of great joy in tangible ways so that others may come to know the wonder and joy of the Savior's birth.

REFLECTION

Do your holiday traditions tend to bend inward or extend outward? How can you intentionally share the hope and encouragement that Jesus brings with the people God has placed in your life? Consider ways you can reflect the love of Jesus through acts of kindness, forgiveness, and service.

PRAYER

Heavenly Father, thank You for showing me the fullness of Your love through Jesus. Thank You for sending Him to be the ultimate sacrifice for my sins. Help me to follow Jesus' example by loving others selflessly. May I live out the love You have shown me and share it with those around me by Your power and might. In Jesus' name, Amen.

24

THE BIRTH OF JESUS

READ LUKE 2:1-7

“In those days a decree went out from Caesar Augustus that all the world should be registered. This was the first registration when Quirinius was governor of Syria. And all went to be registered, each to his own town. And Joseph also went up from Galilee, from the town of Nazareth, to Judea, to the city of David, which is called Bethlehem, because he was of the house and lineage of David, to be registered with Mary, his betrothed, who was with child. And while they were there,

> the time came for her to give birth. And she gave birth to her firstborn son and wrapped him in swaddling cloths and laid him in a manger, because there was no place for them in the inn.
>
> — LUKE 2:1-7

The Savior of the world entered life as we know it in a humble setting in the small town of Bethlehem. This is not how we expect a King to arrive, yet it perfectly reflects the heart of God's plan. He brought salvation, not through an army or dictator, but through love, humility, and sacrifice.

This God-child, born needy and weak, meets all needs for all time in His perfect strength. He pursues our hearts through the cross. He speaks forgiveness in His dying breath and brings life through His resurrection. The Pharisees were not ready, yet they should have known. They had read the prophecies. They had memorized the Word of God, but distracted by tradition; they missed His arrival.

And, so might we.

We can be distracted by the jolly and generous gift-giving at Christmas. Annual traditions and making our lists can divert us from what really matters. As fun as those things are, this is our reminder that the call to find refuge in Jesus will not ring out forever. One day, the lion of Judah, the root of David, the slain Lamb who was born in the manger, died, rose again, and ascended into heaven, will return and collect His own. He will take the scroll and break its seal. He will open the books and judge the living and the dead. He will establish a new heaven and a new earth, a holy city, a new Jerusalem, prepared as a bride for her husband. Because of Him, the dwelling place of God will be with man. The Great I Am is the Son of the Most High and His kingdom will have no end.

Christ has come and Christ is coming again! This is the message of Christmas that began thousands of years ago in the manger. Behold, He will make all things new. He will be called holy—the Son of God. The penalty is paid for those who repent and believe. They can safely enter the presence of the living God and worship Him for all eternity. Thanks be to God for his indescribable gift.[1]

THE BIRTH OF JESUS MARKS THIS ARRIVAL OF HOPE

The long-awaited Messiah fulfills centuries of prophecy, bringing hope to people who had been waiting in darkness. His birth offers hope to us today, reminding us that God is faithful to His promises and that He enters into our brokenness to bring healing and redemption.

THE BIRTH OF JESUS BRINGS PEACE

Though born in a chaotic and noisy world, Jesus brings peace between God and humanity. As we reflect on his humble beginnings, we remember that true peace is found not in earthly circumstances, but in the presence of Jesus.

THE BIRTH OF JESUS BRINGS JOY

The angels announced "good news of great joy" to the shepherds, and that joy is still available to us today. This joy is not found in temporary pleasures, but in the eternal truth that God is with us. The arrival of Christ is the greatest source of joy for all who believe.

THE BIRTH OF JESUS IS A MANIFESTATION OF LOVE

God loved the world so much that He sent His only Son to live among us, to experience human life, and to give His life for us—the ultimate act of love. The depth of God's love is seen not only in Jesus' willingness to come in such a humble form but also in His willingness to lay down His life to redeem us from sin and restore us to the Father.

REFLECTION

Dwell on the themes of hope, peace, joy, and love that are fulfilled in Christ. His arrival on that first Christmas morn, speaks to the heart of God's love for you and His desire to bring light into the darkness. May you carry these truths as you celebrate His birth and look forward to His return.

PRAYER

Heavenly Father, thank You for Jesus, who brings hope, peace, joy, and love to the world. Help me to reflect on the significance of His birth and to live in the light of the promises fulfilled in Him. Fill me with the joy and peace that comes from knowing You, and may I live in anticipation of Christ's return. In Jesus' name, Amen.

25

LOOK UP IN EXPECTATION

READ LUKE 21:25-28

“And there will be signs in sun and moon and stars, and on the earth distress of nations in perplexity because of the roaring of the sea and the waves, people fainting with fear and with foreboding of what is coming on the world. For the powers of the heavens will be shaken. And then they will see the Son of Man coming in a cloud with power and great glory. Now when these things begin to take place, straighten up and raise your heads, because your redemption is drawing near.”

— LUKE 21:25-28

The birth of Jesus was heralded by a star, yet many missed it. How many people were so caught up in their daily routines, burdens, and struggles that they failed to look up and see the sign announcing the arrival of the long-awaited Messiah? They were busy tending to daily responsibilities while the greatest news in history was unfolding in the heavens above.

In the same way, the second coming of Christ will arrive when people least expect it. Just as the angels prepared Mary and Joseph for the miraculous events to come, and the star led the wise men to worship, another heavenly announcement will one day declare Christ's return. But how many will be too preoccupied to notice the signs?

Jesus spoke clearly about His second coming, warning that many would be caught off guard, distracted by "the anxieties of life" (Luke 21:34). The cares and troubles we face today can weigh us down, making us miss the hope that is offered through the promises of Christ. But Jesus calls us to do something different: to "straighten up and raise your heads, because your redemption is drawing near" (v. 28).

Redemption—what a beautiful word for a lost and weary world. It's the message of Christmas: that God stepped into our brokenness to save us. Christ not only came as a baby to redeem us, but He will come again to restore all things. The signs of this coming are not meant to fill us with fear, but with hope. They remind us that our ultimate redemption is near.

This Christmas, lift your eyes above the worries of life and the chaos of the world. Don't let distractions steal your focus. Instead, watch and pray, seeking God's strength and placing your hope in Him. Remember, the same God who sent His Son to live among us is still at work in our hearts today. Christ has come, and Christ will come again. Are you ready? Have you placed your trust in Him, repented and turned from your sin, and embraced the hope, peace, and joy that only He can give? As you celebrate the birth of Christ, let it fill you with renewed anticipation and steadfast hope for His glorious return.[1]

PRAYER

Father, thank You for the promise of redemption and for the gift of hope that comes through Your Son, Jesus. Help me to be watchful and expectant, lifting my eyes from the worries of life to see the signs of Your presence and the promise of Your return. Guard my heart from distractions, and remind me daily that my hope is in You alone. May I stand firm in faith, knowing that my redemption draws near. In Jesus' name, Amen.

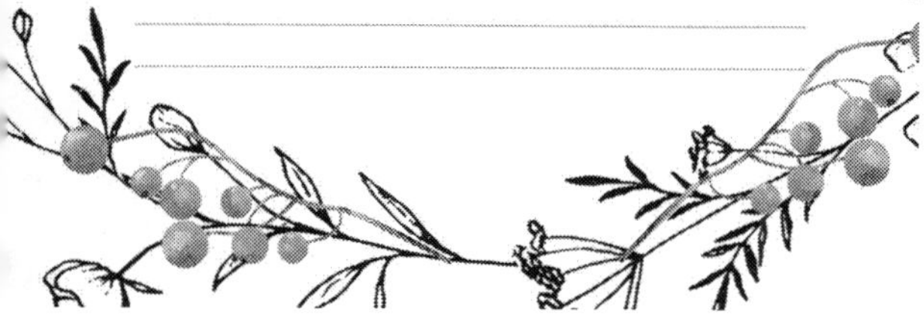

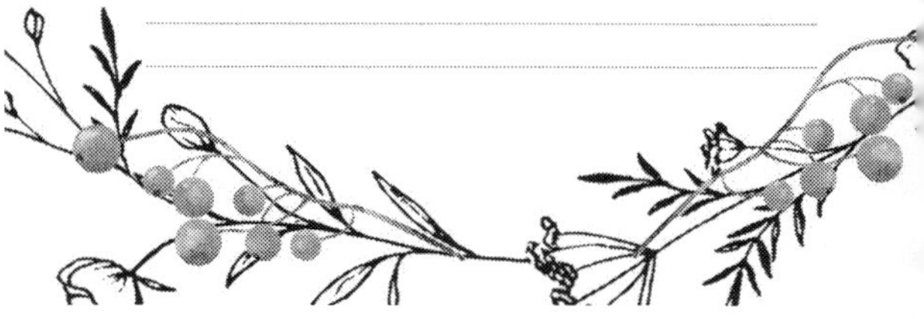

NOTES

3. THE FAITHFULNESS OF GOD

1. A version of this devotional first appeared on StaceyWeeks.com December 2020 and The Great Commission Collective website January 2021.

8. THE PRINCE OF PEACE

1. A version of this devotional first appeared on StaceyWeeks.com May 2022.

10. PEACE WITH GOD

1. A version of this devotional first appeared on StaceyWeeks.com December 2021.

11. ANGELS ANNOUNCE PEACE

1. A version of this devotional first appeared on StaceyWeeks.com December 2023.

12. LIVING IN PEACE

1. An observation shared in a biblical counselling session.

17. JOY IN THE PRESENCE OF JESUS

1. A version of this devotional first appeared on StaceyWeeks.com December 2019.

19. JOY THROUGH THE HOLY SPIRIT

1. A version of this devotional first appeared on StaceyWeeks.com April 2022.

20. JOY IN TRIALS

1. A version of this devotional first appeared on StaceyWeeks.com May 2019.

24. THE BIRTH OF JESUS

1. A version of this devotional first appeared on StaceyWeeks.com December 2019 and 2021.

25. LOOK UP IN EXPECTATION

1. A version of this devotional first appeared on StaceyWeeks.com December 2021.

ABOUT THE AUTHOR

Stacey is a ministry wife, mother of three, and a sipper of hot tea with honey. She loves to open the Word of God and share the hope of Christ with women. She is a multi-award-winning author, a home-educator, and a frequent conference speaker. Stacey has a Graduate Certificate in Women's Ministry and a Graduate Certificate in Biblical Counselling from Heritage College and Seminary.

facebook.com/writerSWeeks
x.com/writerSWeeks
instagram.com/writersweeks

ALSO BY STACEY WEEKS

CHASING HOLINESS

Learn how to live by the power of God and cultivate a lifestyle in keeping with who you really are in Christ.

We all chase something. It might be a degree or career, a spouse and family, the approval of man, or a perception of social success. We long to pursue the things that matter, we long to chase the Lord, but we are weary.

What would happen if we redirected our energy toward developing the character traits and disciplines that Christ calls us to pursue? What if we sought ways to increase our endurance and strengthen our faith? What if we stopped aimlessly running and instead chased the disciplines that would earn the prize that mattered?

Chasing Holiness challenges the status quo level of Christian living accepted for far too long by many today. It's about teaching stubborn hearts through the discipline of seeking God to remain focused on Him. It examines what it means to live by the power of God and believe Him when He calls us his child, chosen, holy, and redeemed. It encourages us to cultivate a lifestyle in keeping with who we really are in Christ. It's an acknowledgment that many of us long to fix our eyes on Jesus and push toward the finish line, but we don't know where to start. Chasing Holiness is about finding out together.

PRAISE FOR CHASING HOLINESS

"Stacey style of writing guides the not-yet believer gently, informs the recent believer, and challenges the mature believer toward the desire for all Christians — holiness ... One isn't left feeling inadequate but rather inspired to chase after holiness as a result of reading this work."

— LAURA COLWELL - FORMER DIRECTOR OF WOMEN'S MINISTRY, HOPE BIBLE CHURCH, OAKVILLE ONTARIO

"There is nothing easy about Stacey's words. This is a clear and necessary call to holy living ... With honesty and transparency, Stacey shares from her own life but not in that I've-got-it-all-figured-out kind of way. The reader will feel the connection and be moved into the chase with her. The book is saturated with Scripture, moving from powerful explanations of the biblical texts to application that is simple and accessible. The study questions at the end of each chapter, Bible study group plan, and list of additional resources make this a must-have book for women who are serious about their walk with Christ."

— TODD DUGARD, LEAD PASTOR - HARVEST BIBLE CHAPEL, BARRIE ONTARIO

"Foundational to Christian living is a proper knowledge of God and responding submissively and completely. This study blends biblical insight with practical reflection to help move us forward in our intimacy with Jesus."

— ANDREA THOM - AUTHOR OF RUTH: REDEEMING THE DARKNESS AND AMOS: COME AWAKE

"Stacey Weeks accurately identifies a massively concerning issue in today's church culture. We long for Jesus but we risk missing Him all together. This is why this timely book is a must read for Christian women who are hungry to grow and faithfully follow Christ. Far too many are missing not just the truth, but literally missing Him! Take Stacey's charge to heart,"He is worthy of pursuing, so Chase Holiness!"

— NORM MILLAR -SENIOR PASTOR - REDEMPTION BIBLE CHAPEL, LONDON ONTARIO

"Paul talks about running the race with endurance, but that can often feel quite ambiguous. Stacey takes you on a journey through the Word of God, helping you ask the right questions; that you might not just "know" the importance of holiness, but understand how to practice, pursue, and even chase holiness intentionally."

— LAURA ZIMMERMAN - DIRECTOR OF PROJECTS AND EVENTS, GREAT COMMISSION COLLECTIVE

"I love this book! I value its conviction. I agree with its goal, and I wholeheartedly support its theology. In a day of *hamster wheel* chaotic lives in pursuit of the temporal, the call to chase after holiness is joyfully welcomed. Actually, desperately needed. Weeks writes with clarity, sincerity and honesty that is easy to digest and then powerfully apply."

— ROBBIE SYMONS, AUTHOR OF PASSION CRY, PASTOR OF HOPE BIBLE CHURCH, OAKVILLE ONTARIO

GLORIOUS SURRENDER

Do you long for the joy of complete dependence on God yet fear the cost of full surrender? Do you long for unconditional acceptance and love but fear exposing your heart? Do you long for solid peace, absolute trust, and contentment amidst alarming circumstances but fear that those circumstances might shatter your soul?

We fight God for control of our lives because we worry that suffering will overwhelm us. We want a future free of risk, hurt, and heartbreak. But God isn't calling us to risk-free lives—He is calling us to surrender. Some of God's greatest blessings are hiding behind those parts of our lives that are most difficult to surrender.

The first edition of Glorious Surrender won the Women's Journey of Faith award. The second edition of Glorious Surrender includes five new personal, in-depth study times in the Word to aid in the application and understanding of Scripture.

PRAISE FOR GLORIOUS SURRENDER

> Stacey writes with transparency about the tension and the transformation that her role as a pastor's wife played in bringing her to the place of ultimate freedom—one who seeks God's glory above all else. She communicates with honesty about the messiness of real life in public ministry, and takes readers on a journey through raw life topics including pride, living authentically, finding true rest in the chaos, and spiritual warfare ... This book is not just for pastors' wives, it is for women wanting to take a vulnerable look at the sins and deceptions that lurk within their minds and hearts that can stall their progress toward finding true purpose.
>
> — ANDREA THOM - AUTHOR OF RUTH: REDEEMING THE DARKNESS AND AMOS: COME AWAKE!

Glorious Surrender is a wonderfully written and passionate call to women. Stacey Weeks has unveiled her own heart and how the Lord has moulded her, broken her, and transformed her through surrender. She shares intimately from her own experience and how it has brought her deep wells of joy.

This book is specifically written with women in mind and therefore is full of insights and wisdom that women of all ages will find deeply relevant. No doubt, you'll be nodding your head as you go through each chapter. Glorious Surrender will renew your mind and touch your heart.

— ROBBIE SYMONS, PASTOR AND AUTHOR OF PASSION CRY

If you want to glorify God in everything you think, say, and do, I recommend reading Glorious Surrender.

— TAMI SWARTZ - BIBLICAL COUNSELLOR

FICTION BY STACEY WEEKS

Fatal Homecoming

The Builder's Reluctant Bride

In Too Deep

SYCAMORE HILL

To Sweet Beginnings in Sycamore Hill

The Sycamore Standoff

His Sycamore Sweetheart

The Sycamore Slopes

One Sycamore Sunday

A Sycamore Secret

MISTLETOE MEADOWS

Mistletoe Melody

Mistletoe Mission

Mistletoe Movie Star

*Mistletoe Meadows Anthology

YOU CAN MAKE A DIFFERENCE

Did you enjoy this book? You can make a difference. Honest reviews of books bring them to the attention of other readers. If you enjoyed this book, I would be grateful if you could spend a few minutes to leave an online review.

- Goodreads
- Bookbub

Manufactured by Amazon.ca
Bolton, ON

41585879R00077